Preservation of Sanity

C.L. Black Jr.

Copyright © 2023 C.L. Black Jr.
All rights reserved
First Edition

Fulton Books
Meadville, PA

Published by Fulton Books 2023

ISBN 979-8-88731-131-9 (paperback)
ISBN 979-8-88731-132-6 (digital)

Printed in the United States of America

CONTENTS

Preface v

Chapter 1: Define Sanity 1

Chapter 2: The Norm 5

Chapter 3: Cycle of Chaos 9

Chapter 4: Self-Sabotage 13

Chapter 5: Game Plan 17

Chapter 6: A Whole New Level 21

Chapter 7: Jar of Honey 25

Chapter 8: War of Attrition 29

Chapter 9: Peace Out 33

Chapter 10: Resilience 37

Chapter 11: Consistent Persistence 41

Chapter 12: Balance 45

PREFACE

In the beginning, others have said we are all born dumb, naked, and speechless. Everything is a learned process; how can it not be, right? Not to say that our chosen or unchosen surroundings are the culprit, but they most certainly play a major role in the foundation or building blocks for our future. Denial is a favorable weapon when someone is challenged regarding behavior that is considered unacceptable.

The problem is we sabotage ourselves, falling victim by consciously and unconsciously engaging in self-destructive behavior, making horrible decisions, and dealing poorly with things out of our control. In other words, we set ourselves up to take ourselves out! Not an ideal plan of action that leads to the attainment of true happiness.

I have heard the expression, "the weather changes, people don't!" What a crock! This is definitely the case if you believe it is, but I'm right here emphatically pleading this very case! Your true self may be bitter at the core, but this does not mean we can't make it a smaller percentage of our postgenetic course we will travel in life.

When reading or listening, please take into consideration that the first five chapters focus on attaining your sanity, chapter 6 is all about sustaining sanity, and the next five chapters focus on retaining your sanity. The final bonus chapter is all about the culmination of your efforts. *Enjoy*!

P

CHAPTER 1

Define Sanity

What is sanity? In its most primitive form, it is defined as "the ability to think and behave in a normal and rational manner." I guess where it gets tricky is, what exactly is considered normal and rational behavior? Sociological norms of course play a major role in defining what is deemed to be *appropriate*. But what happens when subjective nature takes hold and we allow for things to be a bit *grey*?

Wow! What an interesting dilemma we can have regularly by life's doctor on a day-to-day prognosis with no guarantees. Because isn't that really how it is? The goal being to somehow maintain a level of happiness, which is all relative to the amount of sanity we can sustain.

Obviously, not being of sane mind could lead to some type of false happiness due to the lack of understanding and total mindset of an individual. Who really knows what sets the wheels in motion for someone to internally snap and begin mental atrophy? This process that can slowly develop and manifest itself into a type of personality trait.

To be perfectly clear, I'm not referring to someone that may be diagnosed as mentally ill and require therapy and or psychiatric meds. I'm speaking of people that are functional in society relative to their personal sanity that can cause a reflection of the world to become negative. *Unhinged* is a word that comes to mind when we are pushed to our limits of chaos.

This term can definitely be used when the typical day offers up a genuine batch of Mr. Murphy's Lineage! You know, the all-out domino effect life can give at any time for an infinite amount of reasons if you allow for it. Very easy to become a victim and get "caught up" in a damsel of life's carnage.

Who is the one that determines this so-called sanity? The parameters it entails and the boundaries required to preserve are more subjective in nature than most would think. We judge others by their actions, not knowing what the scope of the situation is. And therefore, we can only offer up an opinion that is jaded at best.

Ultimately, it is you that decides what is considered to be sane in your world. As long as you are abiding by the laws set forth and not inflicting harm, the rest is just based on opinion. And I think we all know the saying that applies here regarding everybody having one.

You, and only *you*, have the power to make change work in your favor! It is as simple as that! Of course it will take work, but doesn't everything in life that is worthwhile? This change I speak of is not something that should be taken lightly. Your sanity depends upon the ability to adapt and become one with a situation that requires emotional stability. Therefore, you are not at risk of allowing this to negatively impact your mood or train of thought, which can lead to poor decision-making, which can lead to other problems.

As you can see, your sanity or lack thereof, is extremely important to answering part of life's equation correctly on a daily basis. It has been said the average person will be able to count their true friends in life on one hand. That statement seems kind of "out there" when you hear it for the first time. However, as a tenured veteran in the real contact sport of life, I would have to agree. Having said this, *your sanity should be one of these friends!*

E

CHAPTER 2

The Norm

Sociological norms always seem to make their way to the forefront. Everyone standing in line behind one another as if *leadership* was a death sentence. Very few people understand much less signup for this type of duty because it involves and requires a very scary process known as *self-accountability*! *Your sanity* should be treated no different!

Norms are just what society deems as the right way to conduct yourself in any given situation. Something that is usual, typical, or standard for an individual to use as a guide of behavior. This is very difficult to apply in the realm of sanity because of our ability to independently adapt almost simultaneously between what is expected and what is warranted.

We have to travel outside the norm due to our individualistic nature, and as I have mentioned, this is where it becomes very difficult at times. Who is to say what is right or wrong for you to preserve your sanity? Again, let me reiterate that all things considering, you are abiding by the law, and no harm is being done. The true victory of being sane lies from within.

You are the key to this door of required fulfillment that leads to happiness. "Deep is to hunger, the voice of the genuine, the simmering moment." What this means is that you have to find yourself and make the adjustments to adapt to whatever the surroundings present. Sounds quite easy to accomplish and basic enough that it would require minimal effort, right?

No! On the contrary, it is very difficult indeed to find this place of harmony that exists from within. Most *normal* people think that they have a good bead on life and the everyday *cycle of chaos* it can present. But there is so much more to it than meets the eye and is of relevance.

Society has done well with us in that the training program it has installed is uniform. However, this is not the way I want to deal with my emotional mindset, nor is it the way you should either. This is not some game we are playing here and certainly not a flip-of-a-coin decision.

My sanity has been tested severely over the course of my life in many situations. I have allowed myself to be a *victim* many times at the mercy of others and their lack of sanity. Strenuous relationships and a knack for making bad decisions was a strength of mine. Lessons that I had to endure that have made me the person I am today. Where once I was this so-called *victim,* now I have transformed into an *agent* of change!

Adversity is a whole different world of potential problems life can offer up at any given moment. It can be self-inflicted but most of the time revolves around the challenges life will present. Almost as if it were genetically in our DNA and somehow masterly predetermined. No matter the case, we have to learn and grow from this force of unnatural behavior. Adversity is something that was so prominent in my life it could take the place of my middle name.

It led me to the realization that as soon as we wake up, life already has enough planned for us to deal with that is out of our control. We don't need to complicate it further by doing things that will only be counterproductive. And nobody truly wants this type of outcome when living life to its fullest potential, and maintaining happiness are the hybrid of life! *Don't be the norm*!

R

CHAPTER 3

Cycle of Chaos

The cycle of chaos is something that I refer to as a part of everyday life. It involves acting and reacting in situations that present a chance for turmoil. We all will have to face this *demon of life* and endure it on a regular basis. It will most certainly test us more consistently than one can imagine.

The realization of this is half the battle, much like most things in this world, and being on your "A" game is a must for a positive outcome. The world is in a form of a heightened state of paranoia, and we need to be prepared. I'm in no way trying to freak you out here, but this is just a true statement, and we should be aware of it.

We are all just one bad decision away from being that person you may find repulsive. Remembering who you are and where you came from is a great way to avoid getting *caught up* in behavior that is unnecessary, unacceptable, and basically none of your business! *Your business is to stay grounded!*

Let me clarify, when I refer to who you are and where you came from, I mean the true person down to your core and how far you have progressed. This is crucial in many areas of your life because it tells an all-important mini story of the kind of person you are today.

Knowing this story and being able to retrieve it on a regular basis can be very therapeutic when dealing with periods of chaos. Much like an end-gram, which is a stored pattern we have made from types of practice and repetition. Also, by telling your story in ways others can relate gives you more confidence and reinforcement. Does this make sense?

In my journey through this world of the unknown, I have been introduced to many unconventional situations that have forced an ultimatum. I do not like ultimatums, and obviously this is something that always relies on confrontation. Now I'm really screwed because I'm not hardwired to be an asshole! Most people can just go to their asshole program and push Play. I do not have this capability and have had to really work on my asshole skills to not get bullied mentally.

It is difficult to change your mindset from one extreme to the other and not pay for it emotionally. Too much exposure to this type of behavior can lead to an overload and cause trauma that will lead to some form of PTSD. I know we didn't just face a battle in a real war...or did we? Think about it and develop your own opinion to decide upon.

The fact is that, these battles in the war of life are going to happen within the mind, and there will be PTSD that you have to be prepared to manage! My way of coping and moving on is to stay in the most positive frame of mind possible. As difficult as this may seem, it can be achieved by adhering to the basics when an encounter is presented.

Fundamentally, we should do our very best to not escalate the situation and be sure to encode and decode information in proper fashion. This will eliminate all that is within your control and assure you that the issue is contained. At least from a preemptive stand-point, you are doing the best you can with the information at hand.

And this is all we can do because, surely, we do not have control over the things out of our control, do we? Well, we cannot control others and their intentions, actions, and behaviors, but *we can control the impact it has on us*! Never forget this basic thread of advice, it is not the mindset of "it is what it is," *it is what you make it*!

S

CHAPTER 4

Self-Sabotage

Self-sabotage refers to thought patterns or behaviors that hold you back and prevent you from doing something you want to do. This applies to *all* things that can range from trivial to very important and even the will to live. This is no joking matter, and since everything is a learned process, whatever we practice the most can become a reality.

Is it not true that from an early age we are taught that "practice makes perfect." So why would it not apply to this type of fundamental thought process and learned behavior? It would! The problem is that, we tend to put things on the shelf, so to speak, that we do not understand or may be intimidating and require actual change.

Self-sabotage is like a silent killer stalking its prey of an individual and will not stop until it quenches its thirst for sanity! It is kind of scary when you think about it in this kind of light, but then again, we don't, hence the return of the silent killer. As you can see, exposure to this type of mindset consistently could be lethal and lead to serious issues.

It is very easy to allow for this enemy to creep in on a regular basis because we are so vulnerable most of the time. We tend to get caught up in our busy lifestyles and forget about the very basics in life. If the best offense is a good defense, why are we skipping the defense part? Most likely because offense is considered exciting and more interesting rather than boring defense.

This may be true, but without the boring defense, there would be no offense. Correct? And who says defense can't be exciting and more interesting if we allow for our mindset to entertain this train of thought! We have to be cognizant of our everyday mentality and be aware of all important boundaries that must be in place for a healthy outcome.

The boundaries I'm referring to are the ones we set for ourselves internally. This is different than actual boundaries that are put in place for relationships and things of that nature. It has to do with the way you internally process the negative thoughts that seem to be overwhelmingly endless.

This is *huge* in the sense of development as a *genuine human being* and, at times, will demand a great deal of patience and understanding. The answer is truly within you, but the issue is how do we get to it? We have to develop a personalized plan of action that is going to be effective and attainable. It all starts with taking action and being consistent with protocol that requires self-accountability!

This is something we, as humans, struggle with constantly and look for a way out that is made simple and easy. We all know the real way to true accomplishment is not simple or easy. If it appears that way, then I would proceed with caution! Nothing in my life, meaningful or worthwhile, ever came easy or without a price!

E

CHAPTER 5

Game Plan

How do we *not* focus on these negative thoughts and behaviors and get the best out of life? Well, the answer is quite simple, just keep reading my books and it will all work itself out! In all seriousness, there is some truth to this. Taking the time to read or expose yourself audio-visually to types of positive materials can be a monumental defensive tactic.

The problem is, generally, people do not think they have the time available in what is known as a "crazy busy" schedule. This is where we have to be strong and hold ourselves accountable, if we *truly* want to make a change. Prioritizing is of the utmost importance and developing a mindset of *this is necessary*!

We have to make the time to foster the growth we desire; it is not going to happen on its own. As people have said, "when you pray for rain, you have to deal with the mud too!" So let's deal with the mud! There are worse things in life than trying to better your world by bettering yourself! Believe me, I have done extensive work on myself that has allowed for me to create my own world of positivity.

Anyone can accomplish this by making the decision to *act* on your emotional hard drive and take away its power. What I mean by this is replacing how we feel emotionally with positive power! This will require the replacement of less meaningful behaviors with patterns of substance.

We all want to go through life unscathed and wake up each day brand-new! Who wouldn't? It is in our DNA and grounded much like a defense mechanism—almost camouflaged to the naked mind and very difficult to expose. This is why we have to make a choice to change and become consistent in this change. This allows for conditioning, which will ultimately set forth a permanent transformation.

Start being proactive in nature by holding yourself accountable when doing things you know you shouldn't be doing! All of you know what I'm referring to, and it relies solely on character. Have you ever heard the definition of true character? It is defined as doing the right thing even when no one is around or watching. Basically, acting the same way alone as if you were around anyone else.

This obviously is difficult at times for all of us because we are vulnerable and attacked by many intrusive thoughts when we are alone. Here is where we can take advantage of an opportunity and do something positive to regain this power that lie dormant. Almost as if we are turning on a light switch within our mind and able to see more clearly.

Clarity is a wonderful thing, but we have to commit to the journey by doing these types of positive actions over and over to train our thoughts to become behaviors we want to adopt. Once this happens, growth from within is achieved in a manner in which we can recognize as an actual *benchmark*.

Now we have something to build upon and use for the ultimate goal, which is more happiness, more of the time. This, in turn, will make sanity our best friend and give us that right to preserve something that we have earned, even if based on merit alone!

V

CHAPTER 6

A Whole New Level

What is it like to really understand who you are and what makes you, *you*? Most of us cannot answer this question because of the fact that it requires an actual *creed*. This would be a short narrative of insight, reflecting words of wisdom, to describe the kind of person you are or want to emulate.

This is not an easy assignment, and the ability to complete demonstrates an in-depth calling of *your true will!* We have to really *want* to become better at something and be committed in such a way that it is almost obsessive in nature. There is nothing wrong with the obsession of becoming a better version of yourself!

In most cases, when the term obsessed is used, it is not a favorable situation and may not reflect the best of an individual. Let me be clear and reiterate the fact that we want to become obsessed with being and becoming *a better person*!

The *game plan* I spoke of earlier is quite essential in the advancement to *a whole new level*. It will help develop the kind of mindset needed to complete *your creed* assignment. These words that you create and want to be a standard can be brought to life every time you read them. This is hardcore mental training at its best and is so important to the outcome.

You must be willing to do these types of things that others will not do to achieve the things that others will not achieve. Buying into this fortress of mental toughness is *everything* and hinges on the fundamental rudiments. This can be difficult at times because we tend to want change to happen instantaneous without bearing in mind the required consistency.

Trust me, I know how this works from my own development, and I would consider myself a very resilient person. It is much like setting a goal and challenging yourself incrementally to a point of progress but not overwhelmingly taking us out of the game. We are all playing the same game, just at different levels, and we are all prone to suffering the same fate, just with different devils!

The feelings of belonging on this level with confidence is paramount and is *all* determined again by mindset. To know, trust, and understand yourself is a great feeling when you wake up every day. Even on the days where some would consider the wrong side of the bed, *you* make it the right side!

This we do know is within *your* power, not the power of the unidentified universe and all its boos from the gallery. I completely understand the whole out-of-control dynamics of the world and what I like to call Mr. Murphy's Lineage! Constantly remind yourself of who you are and what you're made of as another defense mechanism for the mental health and conditioning we desire and have earned!

The importance of *you* with respect to *your* world can never be understated. Most of us compare what we mean to others and what others mean to us and overlook the obvious. If you take care of yourself in a manner in which it is truly for the greater good of you, everything else will follow, suit, and fall into place with the universe.

E

CHAPTER 7

Jar of Honey

How do we maintain this high level of expectation from ourselves and deliver one great performance after another on a daily basis? This is a question to explore and be aware of to mesh with consistency. I think one of the most important things we can do at times is give credit where credit is due, hence the jar of honey.

The jar of honey I'm referring to is like an imaginary captured conglomeration of the greatest moments in *your* life. Everything that you feel or have felt a sense of accomplishment falls into this category. This could range from something that would seem trivial to something of greater magnitude. Whatever the case, what matters is the impact it made on you and, of course, the effort invested.

This becomes an important element to the *evolution of the moment* and focusing on the positive outlook it can provide. Most of us have heard the phrase "patting yourself on the back," and in a sense, that is what I'm referring to on a higher platform of development. For example, this would be like taking the time to reflect on where you were at in life at a certain point from ground level in comparison to the present.

This reflection would be very detailed in nature and bring out its finer points. Harnessing the effort put forth and major hurdles that were overcame could be focal points that would resonate and bring this memory to life again. This is crucial in the thought process to negate any stumbling blocks that may be present at the time. Also, positively reinforcing and validating *your will* is a certainty of benefit.

We have to make time for this, even when things seem to be going great; this is when we can become most vulnerable. As humans, we tend to get a bit full of ourselves at times and seem to forget where we came from. This is definitely not a place we want to spend any amount of time in mental captivity.

There is a fine line between giving yourself credit and being overconfident to the point where it is in danger of becoming counterproductive. In other words, use the past experience for future mental fuel and get back to doing what you do to excel! This type of personal reflection is very healthy if used in the right manner and can be such a blessing in times of warranted grace.

Every moment of your life has been instrumental in development and brought you to the place you are this day. *Remember that*! Why not take full advantage of something that was so close to home in your world and use it to build upon? This is so special and subjective in nature that we don't even have to get out of our comfort zones to employ. Of course, the "stirring of the pot" from the past may sting a bit, but for a much greater cause.

This is the type of mental ability that allows you to show just how far you have progressed, and there is so much glory in this realization. These moments have been earned by *you*, and for *you*, on life's battlefield with much sacrifice. Use them wisely and continue to persevere on this quest to stay positive and focused.

R

CHAPTER 8

War of Attrition

The war we face in life will undoubtedly be filled with battles on a daily basis. These mini battles always have attrition of sorts; the key is to limit this as much as possible. When referring to attrition, I mean the rate at which we maintain our equilibrium and, of course, preserve our sanity. How do we minimize this and be prepared to function at our best with a healthy mind?

I'm definitely not going to paint a picture of beauty here and tell you this is as easy as 1, 2, 3. I think it is all relative to each individual and where they currently reside in the mental realm. There are basic steps we all can take to ensure greater probability, but in the end, it all hinges on *your ability* to control the outcome.

Waking up each day with a mindset of, "Don't let the day take you. You take the day," is a great approach! However, this is not always the case when random intrusive thoughts are haunting your mind like some kind of animal stalking eventual prey. We have to snap out of this world of negative value to get to the place we need to be able to start the day mentally fit. Does this make sense?

Dwelling on all our responsibilities and expectations can be overwhelmingly decisive in the cause-and-effect ratio—literally setting us up for a day of just trying to get back to normalcy and obviously infringing on any progress that could have been made. Too many days of this type of behavior pattern can be the culprit of what is known as a setback.

We must maintain a positive attitude at all cost and leave no room for negativity. The world alone has a preemptive plan already in place that guarantees objective failure.

We cannot afford to be an accomplice to such an evil plan! This is why having the right mindset is so crucial to our success each day. My personal opinion is this is as important as the oxygen supply in your body.

I find that if I begin the day with this type of mentality, it usually allows me to ward off most of the thoughts that could have been a deterrent. I definitely think that this is a byproduct of not giving permission and buying into a negative train of thought as we build into our day. We typically find ourselves dealing with whatever presents itself in whatever manner.

This is fine, but we must be preemptive with some kind of defensive scheme to save ourselves from the world that awaits with much out of our control. My friends, this is a reality that we must face and be prepared with our own arsenal. Life is filled with many little secrets that allow for a simpler yet effective tenure here on earth. Why not take advantage of them and become your best version of yourself?

Make your day a "mission of attrition," and do not allow for it to get a foothold on the growth you have earned! I realize there will be obstacles that are real and may take time to work out. What I'm referring to is all the thoughts that, 95 percent of the time, will never amount to anything! Problems that others may have that you care for may fall into this category as well. Be aware of what you can control and take hold of the flame!

A

CHAPTER 9

Peace Out

What people think about you is *not* any of your business! Do you understand what I just said? I want you to really think about this and internalize because it really is an epidemic in this world. Not that it has mysteriously just manifested from thin air, but with the age that we live in and all the "likes and dislikes" on social media, *wow*!

Whatever happened to the days when being liked was of an earned value? Now, it is technically required, or you are exiled from the norm. The more caught up you get with this world, the further you get away from the basic building blocks that make you… *you*! There is nothing wrong with wanting or having these feelings of being liked, but when it turns into a daily mental requirement, this is unhealthy! Much like any other addiction we could encounter in life.

I'm old-school, and I call it like I see it! If you are reading this and think it is a bit overkill, you're in denial! Because it is actually worse than what I'm trying to explain and, by far, the most fundamentally counterproductive function of society right now! Let's break this down on why I feel so strongly about this area of, shall we say, *weakness*.

Everybody wants to feel like a celebrity! Do you know why that is? Because of the way we view them as *better* than all the rest. But we all know that they are human and are liked and disliked as well. We just cannot get past the fact that even if they are disliked, they are still better than us because they are a celebrity. It is pitiful! *Everyone is a celebrity; all it takes is for them to realize it!*

My first book, *The Fundamental Rules for Kindergarten 101* cites related material regarding this very circumstance. This is definitely a mindset, and we all should seek to understand this monumental difference from within. It will change your entire life and the way you live in the present day. This is what I'm referring to as the "peace out."

Making that change is necessary for you to escape from the bounds of society and all that it dictates. Emphatically with no regret saying to yourself, *this is a necessity!* Become the catalyst and *make* the change to *peace out!* Trust and believe in yourself, and you will be amazed at the things you *will* be able to accomplish!

I know you have heard all this type of, shall we say, motivational hype at some point in your life. But why did it not make an impact enough for you to get your ass in gear? Or did it in some way make you at least think about it? No matter the reason, let's do something about it together! You have to commit and make the time to invest in the best possible asset, which is yourself!

Believe it or not, reading this material right now is a sign that you have already begun the transformation you so dearly have earned. No, this is not your subconscious mind speaking to you in different tongues. You are in the reality of making yourself a better person and have taken initiative, which is so valuable, there is no price tag.

Take this attitude into the next day and begin to develop some type of consistency to gain the confidence required for this mental change of circumstance. This has to be top-of-mind awareness so we can adopt a routine of habitual positive reinforcement. Say goodbye to the fake world we live in. You can do this *now!*

N

CHAPTER 10

Resilience

If I had to think of a term that applies to life and the test it presents on a daily basis, it would be *resilience*. I know all of us deep down inside possess this all-important trait that we need to find and grasp hold of at times as if it were some kind of lifeline. Where things can get a bit dicey is determining the amount or level that we may have to access and how.

Some would argue that this may already be decided based on the given situation that arises. I cannot dispute this; however, I do think that it is a hybrid of the situation and the ability to deal with it at any level to preserve your sanity. In other words, we have to be prepared for all encounters and be able to accept, change, and know the difference.

Much like the serenity prayer, which is the following: "God, grant me the serenity to accept the things I cannot change, the courage to change the things I can, and the wisdom to know the difference." For me, this is the ideal prayer, and I think that it is enveloped by *resilience*!

We find ourselves in places of darkness in life that only we are encountering on a level that others may not understand. These are the times of hardship that produce times of grace. On the other side of all the suffering, the slings and arrows of outrageous fortune is something great! But we have to get there!

Being resilient will most certainly be a requirement and become your pillar of stability. I think this is directly related to your *will* and the ability to find out what you're made of on a higher level. There are many things that happen to us that are out of our control. But we do have control over how we deal with them, and this is where resilience plays a major role.

Finding out how we are going to function and move forward through adversity at times is essential in our growth and will define the person we see in this day. There is no escaping the confines of life and all of its testing protocol, but we can be as prepared as possible. This is the point I'm trying to make!

Life can be one big beautiful tragedy that we must encounter, and when it comes to an end, how do you want to be remembered? Maybe I should ask, How do you want to remember yourself? Hopefully, it is for the type of person you have become through honest growth and development.

It would definitely be a disappointment to find out that you lived your whole life the wrong way and suffered from blindness of your true potential. Knowing that you could have been, should have been, and would have been, but you *did not*! Let us not be a casualty of this war of life! Of course, we will fall victim in many battles, but let us win the war!

Be resilient in the face of adversity and challenge yourself to a duel inside the mind that only you have the power to overcome! When fear and doubt creep in, and they will, mentally say to yourself, *Is this really how you are going to allow things to happen?* I know this is easier said than done, especially in extenuating circumstances, but this is why it is imperative that we fiercely condition ourselves!

C

CHAPTER 11

Consistent Persistence

These two words in unison and realized are a dangerous combination of firepower when dealing with life's everyday buffet of adverse conditions. I truly feel that if we can get consistent with anything, the laws of probability dictate a much higher success rate. The key is to make sure that we are being consistent with the *right* thoughts, feelings, sensations, and behaviors!

It can be very easy in this world to get into consistent *irregularity* and become a *victim*, not an *agent*, of change or circumstance. Why do you think there are so many successful criminal minds that focus on evil instead of good? And we ponder, if only these people would use their talents for a good cause, do we not?

Being consistent requires doing things over and over again to achieve a desired result. Much like practice in a sport or on an instrument, repetition will store a pattern known as an end-gram, which we can retrieve at our leisure. Sometimes, this can take longer to develop, depending on the activity or task we seek to employ.

This is where we find persistence and make it our friend. Doing things that most will never do to have things most will never have is the required mindset. With persistent behavior, it is much like blocking out negative thoughts and replacing them with positive actions. Making this action a priority is key in sustaining a cycle of consistency that will lead to our success.

It is difficult to achieve for most because we tend to do these two things separately. For example, we start an exercise routine and begin to develop a consistent pattern, but we fail to plan accordingly when we "hit the wall" or become disinterested. This is where being persistent and making the necessary adjustments to continue in the right direction is crucial.

I know what it's like to wake up every day and wonder, *How in the hell am I going to get through this day?* Not with a mindset of attacking the day, but quite the contrary and allowing fear and doubt to make their appearance with massive entitlement. It is not a good feeling and definitely promotes a level of infectious thoughts, which are debilitating.

Latching on to anything that is of a positive nature is imperative and can be your saving grace many times when we are at risk of falling victim to a day that is just getting started. We must focus on the good in our lives no matter how small or insignificant it may seem to the many challenges that overwhelmingly await.

Mostly everything in our lives revolves around behavioral changes and our ability to adapt accordingly. It all goes back to the fundamentals that are right in front of our faces every day! We tend to overthink and make life more difficult by not taking advantage of these basic mental skills. Do not abandon your ability to overcome these mental obstacles preemptively!

E

CHAPTER 12

Balance

Wow! How do we achieve this elusive path of purpose that seems to be the pinnacle that is never attained? This imaginary place that hails in our minds and brings us peace and happiness, if we can only find it. I think where most people go wrong is they deem this as some sort of treasure hunt. Like maybe it is to be found through opportunities that will eventually reveal themselves and save the day.

When in reality, it's right in front of you, waiting for your blessing and fortitude. The opportunity is created by you from a proactive nature of your own recognition.

We must harness this type of mentality for us to feel accomplished and fill the void of balance. This will allow for improving other areas of our life that are essential to this total equation.

In other words, if we are able to feel at peace in our minds on a daily basis, other forms of behavior seem to fall into place.

I don't care who you are, there will be days of trial that will test your very fiber of being. And we must gravitate to this place in our minds that brings us peace so that we can function at a higher level and still stay in our regimen of balance.

Over the course of time, we will get better and better at developing this voluntary response. And the goal is to transform it into an involuntary response, much like our heartbeat. Consider it as a mindset of a supreme defense mechanism that is ready for action at all times—especially the adverse reality we encounter in certain phases of our lives.

Becoming the best version of yourself will involve a high level of commitment to your mental well-being. Take advantage of any and all opportunities to build on a positive outlook on life. This will help negate many appearances by the world of autonomous fate that defines you. We can only wrap our minds around so much adversity, so why not be prepared to face it and then get a break!

Of course, this break is created by having the knowledge of being able to escape on your own recognizance. This is important because it testifies as to your ability to control the outcome of the impact and maintain a healthy level of sanity. I realize this is difficult to obtain, attain, and sustain—given traumatic events—but I assure you that practice in your daily function of trials will help!

There is a method to all this madness, and keeping *your* sanity right where it belongs is a full-time job! This is serious business, my friends, and one of the primary reasons I decided to write this book. So many of us have no idea how to cope, much less preserve, our sanity, and it has become somewhat of an epidemic. We are all susceptible to becoming a byproduct of negative thoughts and teetering on the brink of madness. Thinking others are somehow immune because of their surface appearance and willingness to bask in it. *Do not buy into it!* Stay true to yourself and invest in ways to spend your time wisely and without objective nature. *Deep down inside, you know who you really are and what you are made of!*

Being preemptive and cognizant of ways to handle the hardships life can serve up on a daily basis is a *must!* Patiently being aggressive with the intent of making your world a better place is the right mindset. Remember, the goal is to be a happy, consistent, persistent, resilient person, and it will definitely all hinge on your ability to act with sanity!

ABOUT THE AUTHOR

C.L. Black Jr. is a tenured and successful business owner who resides in Virginia. He grew up in Baltimore City and graduated from the Milton Hershey School, an orphanage in Pennsylvania. Overcoming adversity and defying the norm have become a habitual sanctuary for Charles. In fact, he would like to submit a formal change for the well-known term "Murphy's Law" to "Murphy's Lineage"!

CPSIA information can be obtained
at www.ICGtesting.com
Printed in the USA
LVHW041525290423
745673LV00001B/330